SECRET
OF THE
BLOODY
HIPPO
... AND MORE!

BY ANA MARÍA RODRÍGUEZ

★ ANIMAL
SECRETS
REVEALED! ★

E **Enslow Publishers, Inc.**
40 Industrial Road
Box 398
Berkeley Heights, NJ 07922
USA

http://www.enslow.com

Acknowledgments

The author would like to express her immense gratitude to all the scientists who have contributed to the "Animal Secrets Revealed!" series. Their comments and photos have been invaluable to the creation of these books.

Library of Congress Cataloging-in-Publication Data

Rodríguez, Ana María, 1958–
  Secret of the bloody hippo— and more! / Ana María Rodríguez.
      p. cm. — (Animal secrets revealed!)
  Summary: "Explains why hippos excrete blood red sweat and details other strange
  abilities of different types of animals"—Provided by publisher.
  Includes bibliographical references and index.
  ISBN-13: 978-0-7660-2958-3
  ISBN-10: 0-7660-2958-1
  1. Mammals—Juvenile literature. 2. Mammals—Research—Juvenile literature. I. Title.
  QL706.2.R63 2009
  599—dc22

                                    2007039481

Printed in the United States of America

10 9 8 7 6 5 4 3 2 1

To Our Readers: We have done our best to make sure all Internet Addresses in this book were active and appropriate when we went to press. However, the author and the publisher have no control over and assume no liability for the material available on those Internet sites or on other Web sites they may link to. Any comments or suggestions can be sent by e-mail to comments@enslow.com or to the address on the back cover.

♻ Enslow Publishers, Inc., is committed to printing our books on recycled paper. The paper in every book contains 10% to 30% post-consumer waste (PCW). The cover board on the outside of each book contains 100% PCW. Our goal is to do our part to help young people and the environment too!

Illustration Credits: Copyright © Jonathan M. Naylor, used with permission, p. 16; Illustration by Celia Strain, p. 14; International Bon Ton Toys B.V., p. 7 ; Jupiterimages Corporation, pp. 10, 18, 22, 24, 29, 31, 37 (bottom); Kimiko Hashimoto, Kyoto Pharmaceutical University, pp. 26, 28; Photograph by Craig Packer, p. 8; Ronald & Dennis Kröger, pp. 35, 37 (top); Ronald Kröger, p. 38.

Cover Illustration: Jupiterimages Corporation.

★ CONTENTS ★

★

ENTER THE WORLD OF ANIMAL SECRETS!

Begin the adventure with the secret behind the bloody hippo—discover why the hippo's mysterious, sticky sweat is something the hippo does not want to wash off. Then visit with the scientist who tried to uncover the secret of a mysterious organ inside the horse's head. Hold your nose as you follow the scientist who found out why it is good for the giraffe to have such a strong scent. Accompany the scientist that combined humongous toys and hard work to find out what the lion's mane is for. In the last stop in this adventure, you will spend time looking into animals' eyes. Join the scientists who discovered why the eyes of carnivores and herbivores are shaped for success.

1

LOOKS ARE THE "MANE" THING

Peyton West was hooked. It was a wonderful idea! People had been wondering about why lions have manes for more than two hundred years. But nobody had the answer. Nobody had gone where lions live in the wild to do the experiments that would answer the question. Now she had decided to find the answer herself.

The "Mane" Plan

West joined a group of scientists who knew lions very well. "It's not an easy project," Dr. Craig Packer warned West when she joined his lab in 1995.[1] Packer knew what he was talking about. He is a lion expert working at the University of Minnesota. He has studied lions in the Serengeti National Park in Tanzania for about thirty years.

During this time, he and his colleagues have collected immense amounts of data about the Serengeti lions. For example, they have learned that the mane's color and length change as the lion grows. They have learned about the lions' health by taking periodic blood samples. And they have followed individual lions over years using radio collars. Joining this group of scientists provided West with a very good head start in her research.[2]

Is It for Protection or to Make a Connection?

When West decided to study why lions have manes, scientists had two hypotheses (untested ideas) to answer the question. Some thought that the mane might work as a shield to protect the lion's body when attacked by other lions. Other scientists thought that the mane might communicate how healthy and strong a lion was to possible mates and rivals. It was also possible that the mane was for both protection and communication.[3]

West first tested the hypothesis that the mane worked as a shield. She reasoned that if the mane's role was to protect the part of the body it covered, then when lions fought, most injuries should be expected to be in that area. West used the thirty-year-old lion records Dr. Packer and others had collected in the Serengeti to answer the question. She studied the descriptions of injuries caused by

> **Meet the Scientists:**
> **Peyton West and Craig Packer are biologists who study how lions behave and communicate with one another.**

other lions. She recorded on which part of the body the injuries were usually inflicted and if the lions had survived the injuries. She discovered that when lions fight, the injuries in the mane area are no more frequent or lethal than the injuries to other parts of the body. The mane area was not a preferred target that would need special protection from lions' sharp teeth, so the mane did not seem to be a shield for fighting.[4]

Toy Lions

So is the lion's mane a signal of the quality of its health and strength? West decided to find out how lions react to one another's manes. How could she do that? She came up with the idea of using toy lions.

West used four slightly larger-than-life stuffed toy lions. She could not find any life-size lions already made, so she sent real mane and fur samples to a Dutch toy manufacturer who made four toy lions. The toy lions had names, too. Romeo had a short, dark mane; Lothario's mane was

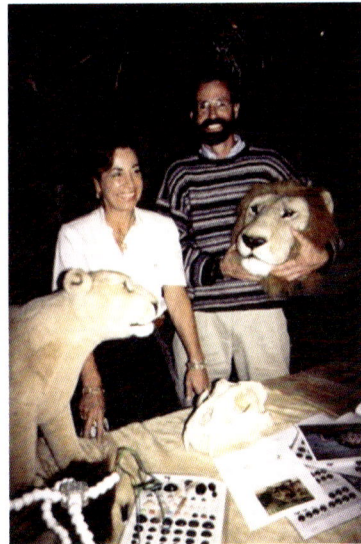

Dutch toy makers used a real-size model of a lion's skull as well as fur samples and photos taken by the researchers in the field to make four real-size replicas of the king of the beasts.

short and blond; Julio's mane was long and dark; and Fabio displayed a long, blond mane. (The manes were attached with Velcro so West could switch them if necessary.) West and the toy lions traveled to the Serengeti to test how real lions would react to the newcomers, Romeo, Lothario, Julio, and Fabio.[5]

Fooling Lions

To test the real lions' reactions to the dummies, West placed two toy lions 4.6 meters (about 15 feet) apart in the tall grasses of the African savanna. To attract the lions' attention, West waited for dusk (when lions are more active) and then broadcast the sounds of hyenas at a kill. When lions hear

A female lion is curious about Romeo, the stuffed lion with a short, black mane.

The lions were fooled, but just once. West was surprised to discover that lions quickly learned to recognize the dummies. Lions that had seen the dummies before—even years before—were never fooled again. They either were not cautious around the dummies or ignored them completely. So to get enough data, West had to travel an area larger than she had anticipated looking for lions that had never seen Lothario, Julio, Fabio, and Romeo before.[6]

these sounds, they move toward them to try to take the kill away from the hyenas.

The lions were fooled. As they approached, they quickly noticed the stuffed "strangers" and immediately shifted their attention away from the food and toward the dummies. They stopped running and became much more cautious. They circled around behind the toy lions, and once they reached one, they sniffed under the tail. To prevent the real lions from detecting the scent of the toy lions from far away, West set up the decoys downwind so the wind would blow the scent away from the real lions.[7]

Looks Are the "Mane" Thing

After three years of displaying the toy lions in the Serengeti, West discovered the secret of the lion's mane. Her results were

fascinating. One of the things she learned was that lions and lionesses responded differently to the stuffed lions.

When lionesses approached the toys, nine out of ten times they moved toward one with a dark mane, not a blond mane. But when males approached the toy lions, in five out of five tests they moved toward one with a blond mane and away from the ones with dark manes.[8]

On the other hand, while female lions did not seem to care about mane length, males moved toward the toy with the shorter mane (Lothario) rather than the one with the longer mane (Fabio) nine out of ten times.[9]

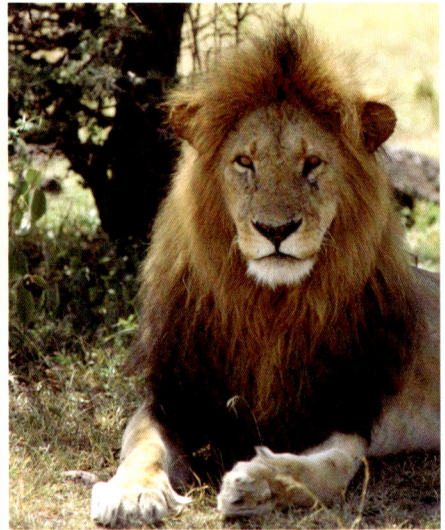

Notice that the mane of the lion at left, above, is lighter in color and less abundant than mane of the lion at right. The mane of the lion on the right is thicker, longer, and much darker, reflecting its good health and strength.

Then West studied lions' photographs and blood samples to evaluate the animals' health. She discovered that the darker the mane, the healthier and stronger the lion, and the longer the mane, the older and less injured the lion.[10]

Lionesses seem to prefer dark-maned mates because they are the strongest and therefore better at fighting off invading lions and defending cubs. Male lions avoid males with dark manes and long manes because they are strong, healthy, and aggressive.

West discovered the age-old secret of why lions have manes. The mane of the king of the beasts is not just for looks—it gives away the lion's worth as a fine mate and a mighty opponent.

> **Science Tongue Twister:**
> *The lion's scientific name is* **Panthera leo.**

GOOD LOOKS HAVE A PRICE

Good looks come at a price. A long, dark mane is like having wool scarves around your neck in the middle of the tropics. Using infrared thermography, which shows the temperature in different parts of the body, West took pictures of male and female lions. She confirmed her suspicions. Lions with dark manes are hotter.[11]

2
THE HORSE'S MYSTERY POUCH

Keith Baptiste has spent many hours studying the bodies of dead horses, especially the organs inside the horse's head. The head holds one of the best-kept horse secrets: the guttural pouches. Since 1756, people have known that the pouches exist, but because they are located inside the horse's head, it has been difficult to study their function in live animals. Their purpose had remained secret more than two hundred fifty years, but not anymore.[1]

An Intriguing Clue

The pouches have a unique structure. They look like small, partially inflated balloons that are about ten centimeters (four inches) in diameter and are bigger at the top than the bottom. Their colorless walls are transparent and as thin as kitchen plastic wrap. The pouches are located just underneath the brain and sit right on top of the throat. They are called guttural because *guttur* means "throat" in Latin.[2]

While observing the pouches in dead horses, Baptiste noticed something intriguing. The main artery that nurtures the brain, called the internal carotid artery, passes right over the pouches before entering the brain. There is direct contact between the paper-thin, transparent walls of the pouches and the walls of the carotid artery.[3] Baptiste was intrigued by the observation.

Meet the Scientists: *Keith Baptiste and his colleagues are Canadian scientists who study horses.*

A "Cool" Idea

In a live horse, the guttural pouches are filled with air that enters the pouches through the throat. Baptiste wondered, How does this close contact with an air-filled, thin pouch affect the blood flowing through the artery? Maybe the pouches help cool the blood.[4]

When horses exercise, they produce heat that warms up their blood. Many scientists thought that if the blood gets too warm, it might damage the brain. Baptiste reasoned that if the pouches cool the blood before it enters the brain, this might help keep the brain from overheating. The pouches might work as blood coolers. Nobody had thought about the pouches this way before.

Baptiste proposed this idea to other scientists and veterinarians in his lab. He showed them the pouches of dead horses, pointing out the close contact between the pouches and the artery. He explained his idea, but many thought he was wrong.[5]

cerebral hemisphere
cerebellum

internal carotid
guttural pouch

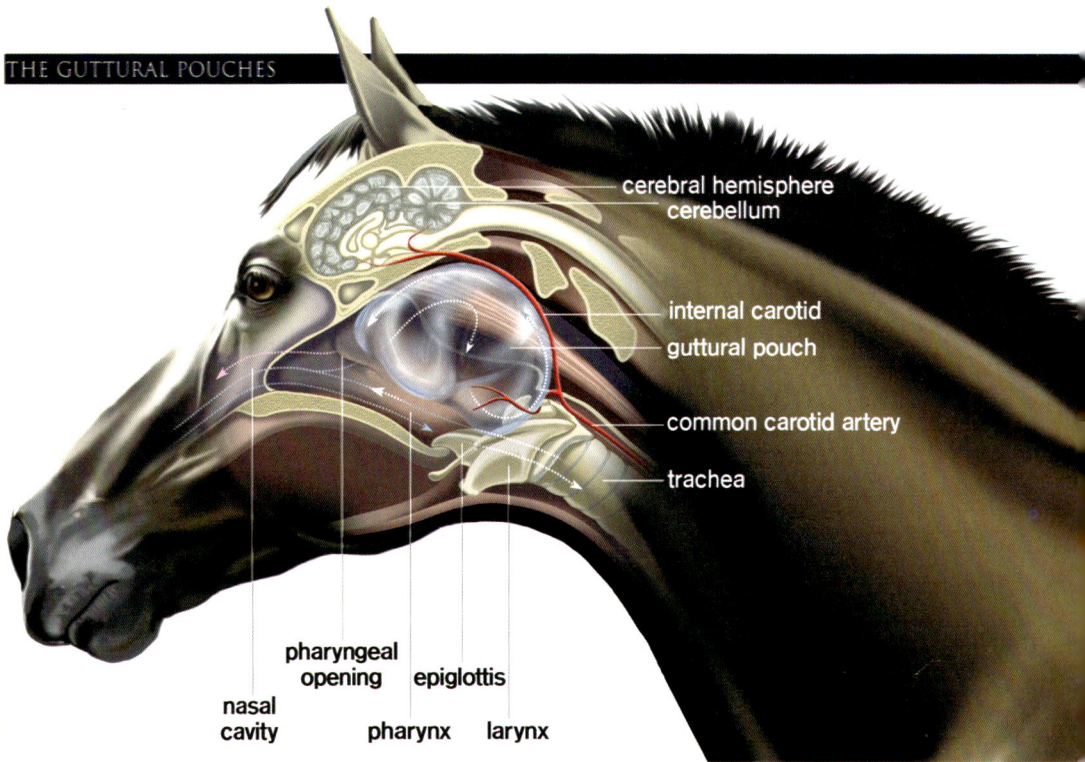

common carotid artery

trachea

pharyngeal
opening   epiglottis
nasal
cavity   pharynx   larynx

The guttural pouches inside a horse's head. Notice the transparent, paper-thin nature of the pouch and that the internal carotid artery rests directly on the pouch on its way to the brain. The arrows indicate the movement of air as the horse breathes.

"Dusk" Brightens the Day

Baptiste's opponents agreed on letting him do one experiment. If the experiment showed that the pouches could work as blood coolers, then he would have the green light to do more experiments to confirm his idea. Otherwise, he would have to find another topic for his research.[6] Baptiste chose a little Arabian horse called Dusk and set him up for the experiment.

First, Baptiste gave anesthesia to Dusk so he would be sleeping while Baptiste performed a special operation on him. He placed specially designed, very tiny thermometers, called thermocouples, in three different locations along Dusk's internal

WELL-CARED-FOR HORSES

After Baptiste finished his experiments, all the horses remained in good health. Baptiste kept one horse for his family, and the others were adopted by other families with children. The horses have a pleasant life in the company of caring children and adults.[7]

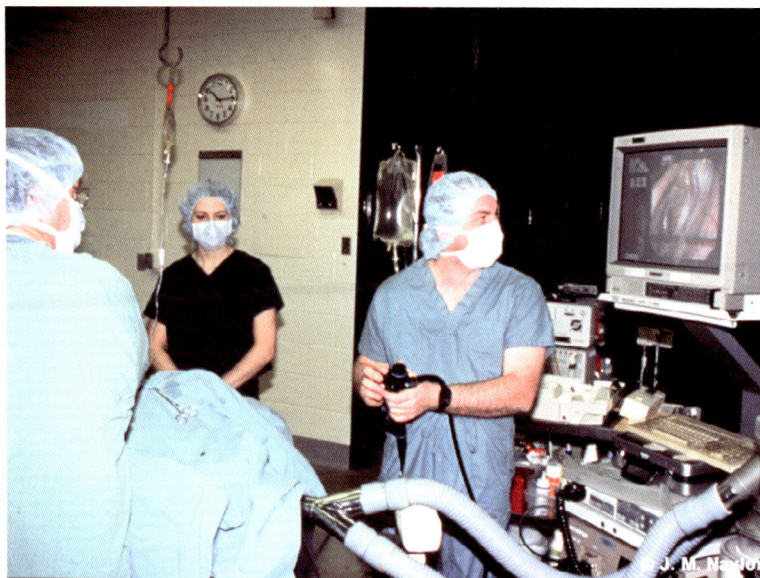

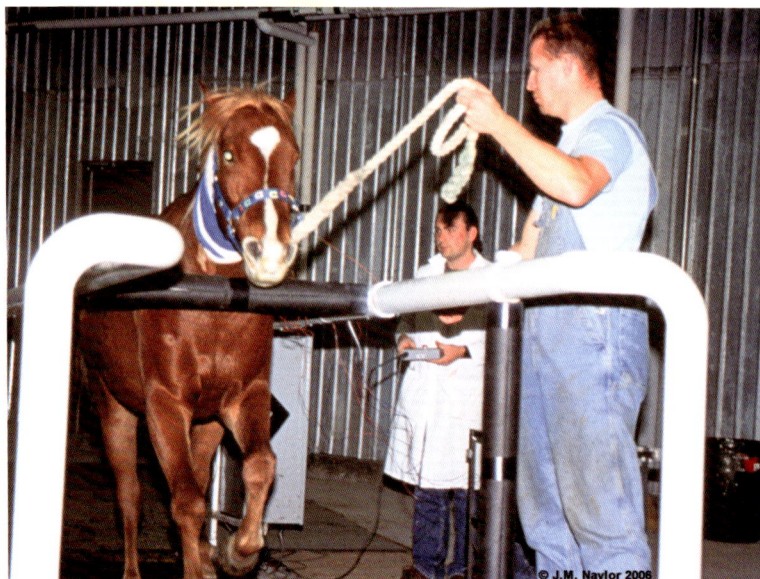

First, Dr. Baptiste (top, center) implanted special hollow tubes, called catheters, fitted with tiny thermometers in the horse's internal carotid artery, which runs over the guttural pouches. Then the horse was placed on a treadmill to exercise (bottom).

carotid artery. The special thermometers would measure the temperature of the blood flowing through the artery. One thermocouple was placed on the artery just before it reached the pouches. The second one was placed on the section of the artery that was in contact with the pouches. The third thermocouple was inserted on the artery close to the point where it exited the pouches, just before it entered the brain.[8] These placements would allow Baptiste to measure the blood temperature before it passed over the pouch, while it was over the pouch, and right after leaving the pouch.

After Dusk recovered from the surgery, Baptiste would measure the blood temperature when Dusk was rested. Then Baptiste would place Dusk on a horse treadmill and have him gallop for several minutes to measure the blood temperature during exercise. This would allow him to know how much the blood temperature changed as Dusk exercised.

The Blood Cooler

The day of the crucial experiment, a dozen people gathered around the barn where Dusk would be running on the treadmill. Dusk got on the treadmill, and Baptiste turned it on while his assistant held Dusk's reins. Dusk began to increase his speed, and Baptiste began recording the blood temperature measured by the tiny thermometers.

> **Science Tongue Twister:**
> *The horse's scientific name is* **Equus caballus.**

Horses in motion. One of the most athletic animals of the Animal Kingdom had a secret within its head.

After Dusk galloped for several minutes, Baptiste had a clear picture of what had happened. When Dusk was resting, the blood in the carotid artery did not change temperature at any point. But as Dusk began to break a sweat, the blood in the artery became warmer before it passed over the pouches. After the blood flowed over the pouches, it had cooled by as much as 2 degrees Celsius (3.6 degrees Fahrenheit). This temperature was comparable to the blood temperature Baptiste and his assistant got when Dusk was resting.[9]

The experiment had proven that the guttural pouches

can cool the blood in the carotid artery. It is not clear yet, though, whether cooling the blood in the artery is enough to keep the brain from overheating during exercise. Scientists continue their experiments to try to answer this question.

Finding the Better Coolant

In this activity you will find out which cools things faster, water or air.

Materials

★ 2 glasses that hold 250 milliliters (about 8 ounces)
★ 2 cylindrical plastic containers wide enough to fit the glasses inside them loosely and at least one and a half times as tall as the glasses
★ meat thermometer with a range -18° to 93°C (0° to 200°F)
★ microwave
★ microwave-safe cup
★ timer
★ an adult to assist you

Procedure

1. Fill one of the cylindrical plastic containers halfway with plain water at room temperature (enough water to cover the height of a glass placed inside the container). Leave the second plastic container empty.
2. Use a microwave-safe cup to warm up enough water in the microwave to fill up the two glasses to 50°C (about 120°F).
3. Fill both glasses a little above halfway and measure the temperature of the water in each glass. Write it down.
4. Place one glass inside the empty plastic container and the other glass inside the one with water and set the timer for 1 minute.

5. After 1 minute, measure the temperature of the water in both glass containers and write it down. Measure again after 2, 4, 8, and 16 minutes. Write down all temperatures.
6. Now measure the temperature in the water inside the plastic container around the glass. Also measure the temperature in the space between the glass and the empty plastic container. Leave the thermometer on the counter and measure the room temperature after 1 minute.
7. Make a chart showing the temperatures of both glass containers versus time.

Observe and Answer
1. Which water cooled faster, the one in the water bath or the one just surrounded by air?
2. By the end of the experiment, how did the temperature of the water around the glass compare with the temperature of the water inside the glass? Was it warmer or cooler, or the same?
3. By the end of the experiment, how did the temperature of the air around the glass compare with the temperature of the water inside the glass? Was it warmer or cooler, or the same?
4. Which is a better coolant, air or water?
5. If you had to cool something quickly, would you use water or air?

3
MESSAGES THAT REEK

William Wood likes to smell things. Actually, his job is to smell things and study the compounds that provide the strong aroma, good or bad. He is a chemist who also teaches at Humboldt State University in Arcata, California. He has studied pleasant smells, such as candylike scents produced by some mushrooms. But he has also studied the stinky scents of skunks, deer, African antelope, and snakes.[1]

Wood has also studied the giraffe. Giraffes produce a strong (and to some, a most unpleasant) scent. Naturally, Wood was curious about what kind of message giraffes were trying to communicate with this strong scent. He headed to Silver Springs Nature Park and Wild Waters Waterpark in Florida to collect the giraffe's scent.

Hair Scents

With the help of his colleague Paul Weldon, Wood collected hairs from two giraffes, one male and one female. Weldon asked the park workers to place each giraffe in a squeeze stall so it would not move. Then he used glass slides like those used to study samples under a microscope to carefully scrape hairs from the neck, back, and shoulder of the giraffe. He collected the hairs in glass vials and froze them so they would

Giraffes approach each other to get a closer look (or sniff). The researchers studied giraffes like these, whose fur is patterned in square-like shapes.

not spoil on their way from Florida to the lab in California.[2]

Once in the lab, Wood and Weldon added a liquid called dichloromethane to the glass vials containing the hairs. This liquid removed the chemicals in the hairs so Wood could analyze them using a special machine. The machine has a tongue-twister name: gas chromatography-mass spectrometer. With this machine, Wood found out how many different chemicals were in the giraffe's hair and how much of each chemical was present.[3]

Stinky Clean

Wood and Weldon discovered that the giraffe's hairs contain eleven major compounds. The main compounds are indole and 3-methyl indole. These smell bad, but Wood and Weldon found out that they are capable of stopping the growth of microbes like fungi and bacteria.

Some of the fungi are the same that cause smelly athlete's foot in people. The chemicals can also attack bacteria like the ones that cause acne on your face. Furthermore, another of the hair compounds is p-cresol, which can repel ticks

Giraffes even "taste" each other in seeking signs of good health.

commonly found in giraffes. Some of the other chemicals are also known to work against fungi and bacteria on the skin.[4]

So what message is the stinky giraffe's scent communicating to other giraffes? The stronger the scent, the larger the amounts of stinky, bug-fighting chemicals, and the fewer the fungi and bacteria the giraffe has on its skin. The more the giraffe stinks, the healthier it is.[5] Wood and Weldon had discovered the secret of the giraffe's strong scent.

4
HIPPO'S "BLOODY" SWEAT

When people long ago saw the red skin of hippopotamuses, they thought hippos sweated real blood. We know that this is a myth. The hippo's "sweat" comes from a different gland than people's sweat. These glands sit deeper inside the hippopatamus's skin than sweat glands in humans do. The "bloody sweat" emerges on the skin's surface through clearly visible holes. When hippopotamuses get hot, a clear, oily, and sticky substance oozes from the pores. This sweat soon changes its color to red, giving hippos their bloody looks.[1]

Hostile Hippos

For many years, scientists could only guess what the bloody sweat was for. One reason for this might be that hippos have a fearful reputation. They may become very aggressive if people get too close to them. Many believe that on their home continent of Africa, hippos kill more people than any other animal.[2]

Because it is not safe to get too close to hippos, scientists studied the sticky scarlet ooze from a distance. Some of them had anticipated that the bloody ooze might work as a sunblock lotion for the hippos. Scientists had on occasion observed albino hippos living under the strong sunlight of Africa among the regular dark-skinned hippos. But the albino hippos did not seem to get as sunburned as would be expected in individuals with extremely light skin. Was the bloody sweat protecting the albino hippos from sunburn?[3]

Other scientists observed that male hippos, called bulls, fight fiercely with one another for territory. During these

Satsuki (the female on the left) and Jiro (the male on the right) rest together. These hippos live at Ueno Zoological Gardens. Their sweat was studied by the researchers. Notice Jiro's large tooth.

fights, hippos slash one another's bodies using their sharp canine teeth, sometimes causing serious wounds. However, the wounds of hippos do not seem to get infected. So perhaps the bloody sweat contained microbe-fighting substances similar to antibiotics.[4]

Japanese scientists led by Kimiko Hashimoto decided to take a closer look. But where could they find friendlier hippos that would let them take a sample of their bloody sweat? Hashimoto and her team headed for the zoo.

Friendlier Hippos

Ueno Zoological Gardens, the oldest zoo in Japan, is the home of Satsuki, a female hippo, and Jiro (pronounced "Hero"), a male. Experts at handling animals, the zookeepers reassured Hashimoto and her team that Satsuki and Jiro were used to the keepers. It would probably

Meet the Scientists: *Kimiko Hashimoto and her colleagues are chemists who study what animal secretions are for.*

be much easier and safer to get sweat samples from Satsuki and Jiro than from wild hippos not used to people.[5]

Hashimoto and her team gave gauze swabs and tubes to the hippo keepers to collect sweat samples. The keepers used the swabs to wipe the hippos' faces and backs once a week for about six months. They stored the samples in special containers and gave them to the scientists for analysis.

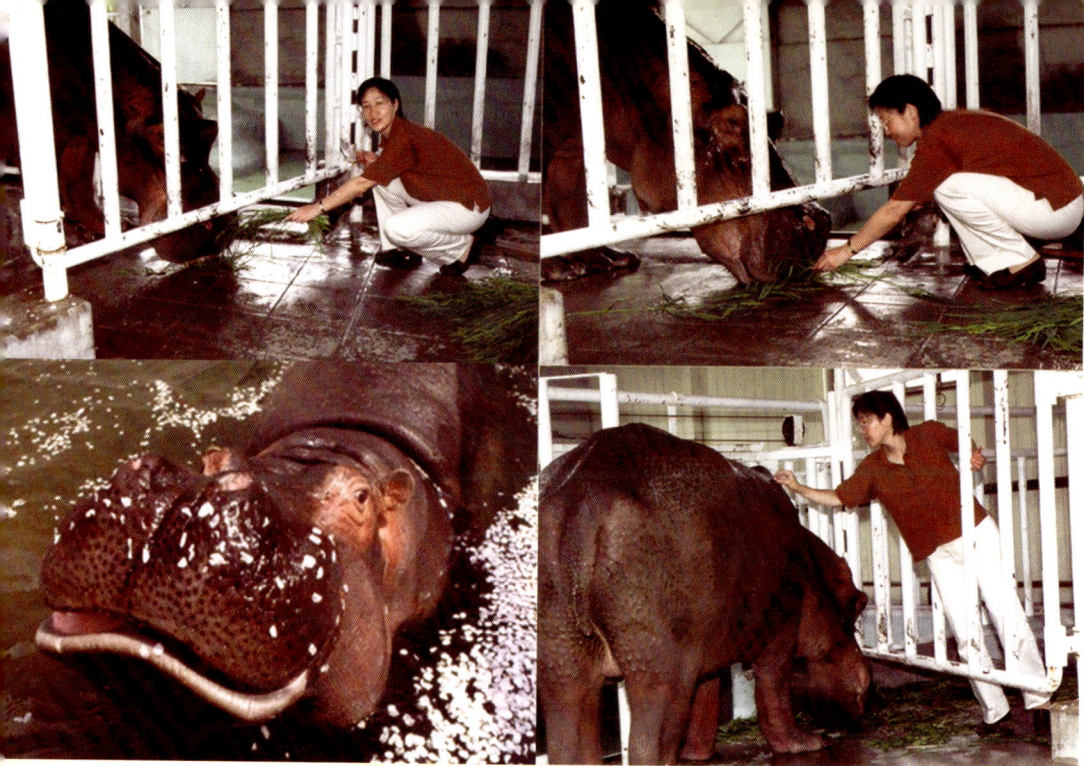

Dr. Hashimoto feeds Naruo, a male hippo living in Kyoto Municipal Zoo (top), before taking a sample of the sweat on its back (bottom right).

Tricky Sweat

In the hands of the scientists, the bloody sweat became a tricky thing to handle. Hashimoto and her colleagues needed the sweat to stay red so they could analyze it and find out which molecules or compounds gave it the red color. But the sweat was very unstable. If it was not kept under the right conditions, it quickly changed color to brown. After much wiping to collect hippo sweat and trying different things in the lab, the scientists discovered that they just had to keep the sweat cool and wet so it would keep its red color longer.[6]

Hippopotami are very large animals that eat plants. Notice the large teeth which male hippos use mainly for fighting other hippos for mates and territory. Also notice the red color on their faces and neck.

Big and Small

Hashimoto's team ran the cool and wet bloody sweat through different experiments to find out what was giving it red color. One of the experiments they did took advantage of the fact that complex substances such as the bloody sweat are usually a mixture of molecules of different sizes. Some molecules might be very large, others very little, and others intermediate in size. So the scientists ran the sweat through a long glass column filled with a special gel that separates molecules by size, like a sieve.

The scientists poured the mixture of molecules into the gel on the top of the column and let it run. As the mixture ran down the column the smaller molecules separated from the larger ones. The larger molecules reached the bottom of the column first and were collected in test tubes. Later, the smaller molecules dripped out of the column. By collecting the smaller and the larger molecules in separate tubes, the scientists separated the molecules of different sizes.[7]

Hashimoto and her team used this technique, called gel filtration, and other techniques to separate the different molecules that make up the hippo's sweat. After many experiments they separated two pigments, or colored molecules: one red and one orange.

The scientists called the red pigment hipposudoric acid and the orange one norhipposudoric acid. The word *hippo* indicates, of course, that the molecules come from the hippopotamus. The word *sudor* comes from the Latin language and means sweat (*Sudor* is also the Spanish word for sweat). Hashimoto and her team moved on to the next question. What do these hippo sweat molecules do?

Double Protection

The scientists first tested if the molecules worked as sunblock. For this they irradiated the molecules with ultraviolet (UV) radiation, the part of sunlight that causes sunburn and sun tan in people. When irradiated, some molecules block UV radiations (and also other types of radiations, like the different colors in light), but other molecules do not.[8] Hashimoto's team discovered that the orange and the red pigments block UV radiations from

Science Tongue Twister:
The scientific name of the hippo is **Hippopotamus amphibius.** *(The name means "river horse," although the hippo seems to be more closely related to pigs).[9]*

The "bloody" sunscreen is visible on the lighter parts of the hippo's skin, like its belly. Even baby hippos are protected.

going through them, just like sunblock lotions. By preventing the UV rays from reaching the skin, the red and orange pigments protect the hippo from the damaging effects of the sun.

Having a self-made sunblock comes in handy to hippos, especially the albino ones. The African environment where they live is extremely sunny most of the year, and they do not have a thick, hairy coat to protect them from the sun. In hippos the red, oily, and sticky ooze protects their skin from the damaging effects of UV light.

The team also tested whether the bloody sweat was like an antibiotic, capable of stopping germs from growing.

HUMONGOUS HIPPOPOTAMUS!

Hippos are really huge animals. A grown hippo may weigh about 3,000 kilograms (about 6,600 pounds). Hippos can be heavier than a sports utility vehicle (SUV). Some SUVs weigh about 2,222 kilograms (4,900 pounds).[10]

When the scientists mixed the orange and red pigments in separate experiments with bacteria that cause serious infections, such as *Pseudomonas aeruginosa*, they were happy to see that the bacteria could not grow.[11]

Hashimoto's team had uncovered the secret of the hippo's bloody sweat. The sticky ooze has at least two uses. It works as a sunscreen and a germ-fighting goo, providing double protection for the frightful, though sometimes friendly, hippopotamus.

5

THE SECRET OF THE SLIT PUPILS

Life in the wild is not easy for carnivores and herbivores. Carnivores have to be good at hunting to satisfy their appetite, and herbivores need to spot predators quickly to avoid being hunted. Imagine carnivores and herbivores, such as crocodiles and deer, that come out at dusk, when light is very dim. They move around easily even though there is little light. Many of them see in color, too. People can barely see their surroundings when it gets dark. How do animals do it?

Slit Pupils

Scientists have looked at different parts of animals' eyes. They have looked at the pupils, which are located at the center of the eye and control the amount of light that enters the eye by opening and closing. Pupils come in many shapes.

The pupils of people, dogs, and tigers are round, but other animals have slit pupils. Some, such as crocodiles, certain snakes and frogs, cats, and foxes, have slit pupils oriented vertically. Other animals, such as some rays, flying frogs, sheep, horses, and hippos, have slit pupils oriented horizontally.[1] Many scientists have been puzzled about this. Why do some animals have slit pupils and others have round pupils? Is having slit pupils better than having round pupils?

Making the Most of Little Light

Most animals with slit pupils are active during dusk or dawn, when there is not much light. It is at this time that carnivores such as crocodiles go hunting for food, and herbivores such as the reindeer need to watch out for their predators. In dim light it is very useful to have a large pupil that allows the eye to perceive as much light as possible. Many carnivores and herbivores active at dusk or dawn have large pupils that constrict to slits in bright light, and many seem to have color vision, too.[2]

Seeing colors through large pupils when there is not much light is a challenge for the eye. In low-light conditions the colors of an object are out of focus. The object appears to have a blue fringe around the edges instead of sharply defined colors. People have called this problem "fringing." Fringing is not just a problem for dusk creatures with color vision. It also

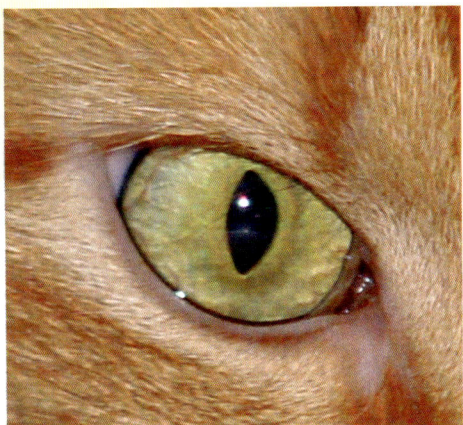

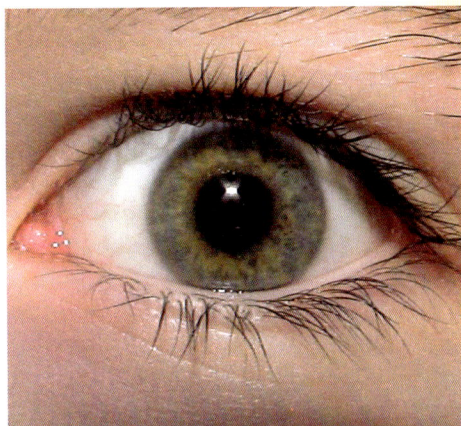

Left: Close-up of a cat's pupil. Notice the pupil has the shape of a vertical slit. Right: Tina, the daughter of the researcher studying animal pupils, volunteered her round pupil for comparison with the other animal pupils.

affects man-made optical instruments such as cameras and microscopes.[3]

To fix the problem of out-of-focus colors, people have made special lenses that focus red, blue, and green at about the same point, so all the colors look focused. Scientists have wondered if creatures that are active at dusk have also come up with a way to correct for color fringing to see better in dim light. Ronald Kröger and his colleagues discovered that they have.

Wavy Lenses

Kröger works at Lund University in Sweden where he and his colleagues study animal eye designs. Besides studying pupils' shapes, Kröger and his colleagues have studied how animal eye lenses help focus colors in dim light. Eye lenses are clear structures behind the pupils that focus images on the back of the eye. The scientists began studying fish, which can see in color, many of whom live in waters with little light.

Kröger and his colleagues discovered that fish have special lenses that correct the problem of color fringing. Fish lenses can focus red, green, and blue light at the same point, so colors look more focused to the fish. When scientists inspected fish lenses very closely, they saw that the lenses have ringlike, or wavy, profiles.[4] The rings, or waves, look like concentric circles on the lens. In comparison, animals that do not see colors in dim light have smooth lenses instead of wavy ones.

Meet the Scientists: *Ronald Kröger and Tim Malmström are biologists interested in understanding how the eyes of animals living in different environments work.*

After studying fishes' eyes, Kröger and his student Tim Malmström wondered if the eyes of land carnivores and herbivores active when the light is dim were also capable of focusing colors. To answer this question, the scientists took out their cameras and headed for the zoo and their own backyards.

Taking Pictures

Kröger and Malmström took pictures of the eyes of twenty different species. They took pictures of the pupils and also of the lenses inside the animals' eyes.

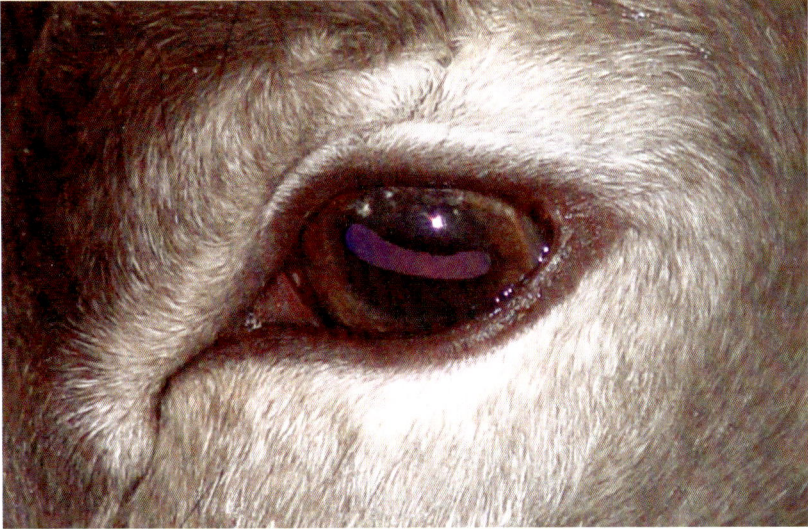

Top: Close-up of a reindeer's pupil. See that it has the shape of a horizontal flattened disc. Bottom: This frog has a vertical slit pupil, just like the cat's pupil.

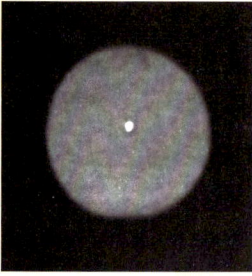

Infrared snapshots of a boy's lens (top, Dr. Kröger's son) and a loris's lens (a loris is a small nocturnal primate with large eyes). Notice that the human lens has a smooth surface, indicating its monofocal nature, while the loris's lens has a ring-like, or wavy, profile which indicates its multifocal nature.

To take pictures of the eye lenses, the scientists used a digital camera that is sensitive to infrared light (this light is invisible to our eyes, but can be detected with night vision goggles). They took pictures from up to 2 meters (6.6 feet) away from the animal and in dim light conditions. If they had used a bright light instead, the pupil would have closed and covered the lens (closing the pupil in bright light is a reflex, or automatic response, of the eye).

If the infrared picture of the lens showed concentric rings, then the lens would probably be able to focus colors in dim light conditions. However, if the picture of the lens looked like one smooth circle, then the lens would not be able to focus colors in dim light, causing fringing.[5]

To take close-up pictures of the animals' pupils, the scientists used a regular digital camera. The results were clear. All the carnivores and herbivores that had slit pupils also had lenses with concentric rings (meaning they could focus colors

CARNIVORE AND HERBIVORE EYES

Vision is a very important sense for many carnivores and herbivores, and each type of animal has a different eye design to help it survive. Herbivores have both eyes to the sides of their heads. This provides them with a wide field of vision, which lets them see predators that are at their sides and sometimes behind them without turning their heads.

A carnivore, on the other hand, has both eyes located toward the front of the head. This allows both eyes to focus on an object with the depth perception needed to determine the distance to its prey.

in dim light).[6] Now they wondered why having a slit pupil is better than having a round pupil to focus colors.

It Is All in the Shape

After much thinking, Kröger and Malmström came up with an explanation for the slit pupil. The pupil is located in front of the lens. As it closes, it blocks more and more light, so less and less light will cross the lens.

When the pupil is fully opened, or dilated, whether it is round or slit, all the areas of the lens can be used to focus light. In a lens with concentric rings, the outer ring will, for example, focus blue, the center ring will focus green, and the concentric area in between will focus red. Other combinations of colors are also possible, and many animals can even detect and focus ultraviolet (UV) light.[7]

When a round pupil closes, it covers the outer area of the lens, so the blue color cannot be focused. On the other hand, when a slit pupil closes, all concentric areas of the lens can be used and all colors are focused.[8]

The mystery of the slit pupils was solved. Carnivores and herbivores with slit pupils have special lenses, and this combination helps them focus colors in both dim and bright light. Next time you go to the zoo or just to your backyard, take a look at animals' eyes. If you see slit pupils, then you know that unlike your eyes, these eyes allow the animal to see colors when you see only shadows.

How Slit Pupils Work

This activity will show you how slit pupils help animals with "wavy" lenses take advantage of their intriguing lens design to see colors in both dim and bright light.

Materials

★ construction paper or poster board in four colors: dark gray, blue, red, and green
★ scissors
★ ruler
★ compass

Procedure

1. Using the ruler and the compass, draw a circle with a diameter of 20 centimeters (8 inches) on the gray paper and cut it out.
2. In the same way, draw and cut a circle 15 centimeters (6 inches) in diameter from the blue paper.
3. Draw and cut a circle 10 centimeters (4 inches) in diameter from the red paper.
4. Draw and cut a circle 5 centimeters (2 inches) in diameter from the green paper.
5. Place these circles on top of one another in the following order: gray first, then the blue circle centered on top of the gray, followed by the red, and finally the green. This represents a model of an open pupil (gray circle) and a wavy lens in which each concentric circle would focus a different color.

Create a partially closed round pupil:

Draw and cut a circle 20 centimeters (8 inches) in diameter from the gray paper. In this circle, draw a centered circle 15 centimeters (6 inches) in diameter. Cut it out and discard it.

Create a partially closed slit pupil:

Draw and cut a circle 20 centimeters (8 inches) in diameter from the gray paper. In this circle, draw an oval in the center.

Make the oval 15 centimeters (6 inches) long and 8 centimeters (about 3 inches) wide. Cut it out and discard it.

See how pupils of different shapes affect the use of wavy lenses:

1. Place the model of a partially closed round pupil on top of the model of the wavy lens. How many areas of the lens are not covered by the partially closed round pupil? How many colors can the lens focus?

2. Place the model of the partially-closed slit pupil on top of the wavy lens model, longer axis vertically (remove the partially closed round pupil first). How many areas of the lens can you see? How many colors can the lens focus?

3. Rotate the slit pupil model so the longer axis is now horizontal. How many areas of the lens can you see? How many colors can the lens focus?

★ CHAPTER NOTES ★

Chapter 1. Looks are the "Mane" Thing

1. Peyton West, "The Lion's Mane," *American Scientist*, Vol. 93, No. 3, May/June 2005, pp. 226–235.
2. Ibid., p. 227.
3. Peyton West and Craig Packer, "Sexual Selection, Temperature, and the Lion's Mane," *Science*, Vol. 297, No. 5585, August 23, 2002, pp. 1339–1343.
4. Ibid., p. 1339.
5. Ibid., p. 1340.
6. Personal interview with Dr. Peyton West, January 19, 2007.
7. Ibid.
8. Peyton West and Craig Packer, p. 1340.
9. Ibid., p. 1341.
10. Personal interview with Dr. Peyton West.
11. Peyton West and Craig Packer, p. 1340; Greg Breining, "The Lion King," *Minnesota Magazine*, March/April 2005, <http://www.alumni.umn.edu/23Feb20052.html> (September 13, 2007)

Chapter 2. The Horse's Mystery Pouch

1. Keith Baptiste, "A Preliminary Study of the Role of the Equine Guttural Pouches in Selective Brain Cooling," *The Veterinary Journal*, Vol. 155, No. 2, March 1998, pp. 139–148.
2. Keith Baptiste, et al., "A Function for Guttural Pouches in the Horse," *Nature*, Vol. 403, No. 6768, January 27, 2000, pp. 382–383.
3. Keith Baptiste, "Functional Anatomy Observations of the Pharyngeal Orifice in the Equine Guttural Pouch (auditory tube diverticulum)," *The Veterinary Journal*, Vol. 153, No. 3, May 1997, pp. 311–319.

4. Keith Baptiste, et. al., "A Function for Guttural Pouches in the Horse," p. 382.

5. Personal interview with Dr. Keith Baptiste, November 1, 2000.

6. Ibid.

7. Ibid.

8. Keith Baptiste, "A Function for Guttural Pouches in the Horse," p. 382.

9. Ibid.

Chapter 3. Messages That Reek

1. Dr. William F. Wood's Web site, September 1, 2005, <http://www.humboldt.edu/~wfw2/home.shtml> (September 13, 2007).

2. William Wood and Paul Weldon, "The Scent of the Reticulated Giraffe (*Giraffa camelopardalis reticulata*)," *Biochemical Systematics and Ecology*, Vol. 30, No. 10, November 2002, pp. 913–917.

3. Rachel Shermeta Pepling, "Critter Chemistry, Stinky, Yet Sexy. Giraffe's Rank Smell May Repel Pests and Attract Mates," *Chemical and Engineering News*, July 7, 2003, <http://pubs.acs.org/cen/science/8127/8127giraffes.html> (September 13, 2007).

4. Wood and Weldon, p. 914.

5. Ibid.

Chapter 4. Hippo's "Bloody" Sweat

1. Yoko Saokawa, Kimiko Hashimoto, et al., "Pigment Chemistry: The Red Sweat of the Hippopotamus," *Nature*, Vol. 429, No. 6990, May 27, 2004, p. 363.

2. Joseph Dudley, "Reports of Carnivory by the Common Hippo *Hippopotamus amphibious*," *South African Journal of Wildlife Research*, Vol. 28, No. 2, 1998, pp. 58–59.

3. Personal interview with Dr. Kimiko Hashimoto, January 30, 2007.

4. Ibid.

5. Ibid.

6. Yoko Saokawa, Kimiko Hashimoto, et al., p. 363.

7. Ibid.

8. Louisa Wray Dalton, "Hippos Sweat Protection," *Chemical and Engineering News*, May 31, 2004, <http://pubs.acs.org/cen/news/8222/8222notw9.html> (September 13, 2007).

9. Kart Benirschke, "East African River Hippopotamus, Pygmy Hippopotamus," University of California, San Diego, School of Medicine Web site, June 2007, <http://medicine.ucsd.edu/cpa/hippo.html> (September 17).

10. Ibid.

11. Yoko Saokawa, Kimiko Hashimoto, et al., p. 363.

Chapter 5. The Secret of the Slit Pupils

1. Tim Malmström and Ronald Kröger, "Pupil Shapes and Lens Optics in the Eyes of Terrestrial Vertebrates," *The Journal of Experimental Biology*, Vol. 209, 2006, pp. 18–25.

2. I. R. Schwab and N. Hart, "More Than Black and White," *British Journal of Ophthalmology*, Vol. 90, 2006, p. 406.

3. Ronald Kröger, "Multifocal Lenses Compensate for Chromatic Defocus in Vertebrate Eyes," *Journal of Comparative Physiology A*, Vol. 184, 1999, pp. 361–369.

4. Ibid., p. 363.

5. Tim Malmström and Ronald Kröger, p. 20.

6. Personal interview with Dr. Ronald Kröger, February 2, 2007.

7. Ibid.

8. Tim Malmström and Ronald Kröger, p. 23.

★ GLOSSARY ★

albino ★ A person or animal whose skin and hair are pale or white due to a lack of pigmentation and whose irises are pink.

anesthesia ★ A drug that causes loss of pain.

antibiotic ★ A substance that kills or inactivates bacteria in the body.

artery ★ The type of blood vessel that carries blood from the heart to the rest of the body.

carnivore ★ An animal that eats other animals.

concentric ★ The quality of sharing the same center.

constrict ★ To make something narrower.

fungi ★ Single-celled organisms that live by absorbing nutrients from dead matter.

gland ★ An organ that produces or removes substances from the body.

herbivore ★ An animal that eats mostly plants and grass.

hypothesis ★ An unproven explanation for a phenomenon.

pupil ★ The dark opening at the center of the eye's iris.

radio collar ★ Tagging device placed on animals to track their whereabouts.

thermocouple ★ A device to measure temperature.

thermography ★ The recording of a visual image of the heat produced by a body.

★ FURTHER READING ★

Books

Anderson, Jill. *Giraffes*. Minnetonka, Minn.: NorthWord, 2005.

Crisp, Marty. *Everything Horse: What Kids Really Want to Know About Horses*. Minnetonka, Minn.: NorthWord, 2005.

Perkins, Wendy. *Animal Eyes*. Mankato, Minn.: Capstone Press, 2007.

Squire, Ann. *Lions*. New York: Children's Press, 2005.

Storad, Conrad. *Hippos*. Minneapolis, Minn.: Lerner Publishers, 2005.

Internet Addresses

Lion Research Center, University of Minnesota
http://www.lionresearch.org/main.html

Silent Sentinals? Find Out How Giraffes Communicate
http://www.pbs.org/wnet/nature/tallblondes/infrasound.html

Mammals: Hippopotamus
http://www.sandiegozoo.org/animalbytes/t-hippopotamus.html

Eye, Eye, Eye, Eye: Questions About Eyes
http://ebiomedia.com/gall/eyes/eye1.html

Ana Maria Rodriguez's Homepage
http://www.anamariarodriguez.com

★ INDEX ★